GUIDED SCIENCE READERS

Animals
Teaching Guide

Lessons, Activities & Reproducible Pages
for Building Essential Literacy Skills

NEW YORK • TORONTO • LONDON • AUCKLAND • SYDNEY
MEXICO CITY • NEW DELHI • HONG KONG • BUENOS AIRES

Photos © 2012: Alamy Images: 28 (Picture Press), 32 (Reinhard Dirscherl); iStockphoto: 22 (Alxpin), 25 (Ameng Wu), 2 top left, 31 (Anna Utekhina), 26 (Antagain), 4, 33 (Bart Sadowski), 2 top right, 21, 38 (Eric Isselée), 35 (Horst Puschmann), 2 bottom (narvikk), 19 (Nathan Gilder), 5, 20 (rusm), 17 (Trout55), 16 (Valeriy Kirsanov); Photo Researchers/Maurizio Valentini: 30; Scholastic, Inc.: covers throughout; Shutterstock, Inc.: 24 (Bogdan Ionescu), 23 left (Dusan Zidar), 36 (Ingrid Petitjean), 23 right (Peter Kirillov).

Scholastic grants teachers permission to photocopy the reproducible pages from this book for room use. No other part of this publication may be reproduced in whole or in part, or stored in a retrieval system, or transmitted in any form or by any means, electronic, mechanical, photocopying, recording, or otherwise, without permission of the publisher. For information regarding permission, write to Scholastic Teaching Resources, 524 Broadway, New York, NY 10012-3999.

Design by Maria Lilja
Illustrations by Doug Jones

Product ISBN: 978-0-545-44272-5

Copyright © 2012 by Lefty's Editorial Services

All rights reserved. Printed in China.

Contents

Introduction 4
What's Inside 6
Tips for Using *Guided Science Readers* 8
Sample Lesson 9
Assessment 10
Graphic Organizers 11

Book-by-Book Reproducibles

Bat Facts Reproducible 16
Beautiful Butterflies Reproducible 17
Hello, Whale! Reproducible 18
A Frog Grows Up Reproducible 19
Penguins Can Go! Reproducible 20
Wolf Countdown Reproducible 21
Fish Live There! Reproducible 22
Meet Some Mammals Reproducible 23
Swim, Hop, Crawl Reproducible 24
See the Reptiles Reproducible 25
That Bug! Reproducible 26
There Is a Bird Reproducible 27
Desert Animals Reproducible 28
Farm Friends Reproducible 29
Forest Animals Reproducible 30
The Icy, Cold Arctic Reproducible 31
In a Coral Reef Reproducible 32
I Spy a Rain Forest Reproducible 33
Animal Stars Reproducible 34
Chicken Life Cycle Reproducible 35
Copycat Critters Reproducible 36
Night Animals Reproducible 37
Tails, Tails, Tails! Reproducible 38
Who Is Hiding? Reproducible 39

Animal Shape Templates 40

Introduction

Welcome to *Guided Science Readers*, a set of 24 engaging nonfiction titles sure to reach each and every child in your classroom—from the most emergent readers to those with higher-level literacy skills. The books are designed to line up with the first four guided reading levels. You'll find six titles at each level: A, B, C, and D, which allows children to step up into harder texts as they acquire new skills. If you already have a guided-reading program in your classroom, the books will integrate seamlessly—you get six copies of each title, making them perfect for small-group lessons. If not, *Guided Science Readers* provide a perfect vehicle to start one!

Plus, *Guided Science Readers* are unique in that they provide children with a way to explore nonfiction—a genre that's important to introduce early in their school experience. Reading informational text prepares children for the kinds of learning they'll need to do as they move up through the grades, and *Guided Science Readers* immerse children in essential nonfiction—a core standard. The books also focus on high-interest topics children naturally gravitate toward—animals, where they live, and what they do. Add in gorgeous, full-color photographs, and you've got books that children will want to read over and over again!

Guided Reading With *Guided Science Readers*

At Level A, *Guided Science Readers* are designed to support children in the emergent stage of reading. At Levels B, C, and D, the books provide you with tools to support readers with a little more experience under their belts at each stage. Children are motivated to read more when they're given books that are "just right" for their reading level. This means that they are able to understand most of the text on their own. It also means that when children encounter new or unfamiliar words, they are able to decode most of them by themselves, using strategies they've already learned and can use independently, or with just a little bit of scaffolding. "Just right" books give children confidence, which sets the stage for increased fluency and comprehension.

To that end, *Guided Science Readers* include the following essential features:

- limited text on each page (one to three lines)
- highly supportive photographs that closely match the text
- patterned text structure
- natural syntactic structures
- repeated and recognizable high-frequency words
- consistent print placement

If children read too many "easy" books, it may inhibit their literacy development; and if they read too many "hard" books, it may lead to frustration. But repeated experiences with books that provide just the right amount of success and challenge gives children the opportunity to both develop and practice the essential skills they need to become better readers. These critical reading strategies include:

- noticing language patterns and style of the text
- figuring out unfamiliar words by using decoding skills to sound out words and context clues to confirm word meanings
- returning to the text to confirm understanding
- connecting the text to other texts and their own experiences
- forming opinions about the books they have read

When children develop these skills, they've got the tools they need to graduate to more and more challenging titles—and the earlier they start building up that toolbox, the better! *Guided Science Readers* is here to help children climb the ladder to reading success.

Teaching Nonfiction With *Guided Science Readers*

While many assume that children naturally prefer storybooks over other kinds of texts, research has proven this to be untrue. Children are naturally curious about the world around them, and will often self-select books to help them find out more. Good reading habits are, of course, developed by catering to children's natural interests, but it's also important to think about the specific skills children gain from immersion in nonfiction material. Here are just a few benefits you'll find from using *Guided Science Readers* in the classroom:

They build vocabulary. Nonfiction and informational text exposes children to vocabulary they may not encounter in storybooks or in everyday conversation. Content area reading, such as science, introduces children to words like *tadpole, mammal, scales,* and even *salamander*! Learning these words in context makes them more concrete, and reading them repeatedly helps make them part of children's own vocabulary over time.

They increase content knowledge. Children learn much about the world through their own experience. However, nonfiction texts increase that experience by giving children world knowledge they are not likely to encounter on their own. Children may never visit a real rain forest, but by reading *I Spy a Rain Forest,* they'll know what they'd find there if they did!

They help set the stage for academic achievement. As children move up through the grades, they will be faced with increasing amounts of nonfiction text. Teaching nonfiction early prepares children for this. When they first come to school, children must learn to read. Once they master that, they start reading texts to learn. *Guided Science Readers* help children gain experience in doing both at once!

Guided Science Readers, along with the tools in this guide, will provide you with a flexible resource for both literacy and content learning—all at your fingertips. Enjoy!

What's Inside

Here's a quick tour of the components included in your *Guided Science Readers* set—and the many ways to use each one!

The Readers

Inside the handy storage tub, you'll find six titles each at four successive guided reading levels: A, B, C, and D. There are six copies of each title, for a total of a whopping 144 books! The differentiated levels not only allow you to find on-level books for each child, but also allow students at lower levels to move up to the higher ones as they acquire new skills. Plus, the cohesive nonfiction topics mean that each time students complete a level, they have also completed a science unit on animals! And with so many copies, there are a wide variety of ways to use these little books. You can:

- use them in small-group guided reading lessons
- place them in leveled tubs as selections for independent reading
- send them home for families to read with their children
- record a reading and place them in a listening center for independent practice
- use them as resources for animal units
- and much more!

Graphic Organizers

On pages 11–15 of this guide, you'll find five reproducible graphic organizers to boost comprehension and help children get the most out of reading nonfiction. They can be used with almost any book in the set as follows:

T-Chart This super-flexible chart can be used in many ways. For instance, list vocabulary words on the left and their meanings on the right. List questions or predictions on the left, and answers on the right. Children might even write an animal's name on the left and draw a small picture on the right.

Idea Web This classic organizer is great for jotting ideas about a central subject. For instance, you might write *Penguins* in the center, and facts such as *can hop, can slide, can dive*, and so on in the outer circles.

Venn Diagram Use this diagram to compare two different animals. For instance, children might note in one circle that pigs say "oink," in the other that lambs say "baa," and in the center that both live on a farm.

Main Idea and Details This organizer is great for helping children focus on central information. Help them find the main idea of a book and note it in the top box (for instance, *Fish live in many places*). Then help them find the details and write one in each box (in this case, *fish live in rivers; fish live in lakes; fish live in oceans*).

KWL Chart Use this chart before and after reading to track children's learning process. In the first column, tap prior knowledge by listing what children already know about the given topic. In the second, pique their curiosity by asking and jotting down what they want to find out. Then, after reading, make the experience concrete by having them reiterate what they learned.

Book-by-Book Reproducibles

Starting on page 16, you'll find an individual reproducible activity sheet for each title in the set. These simple draw-and-write prompts give children a chance to respond to the book at their own skill level. The directions are simple, allowing you to leave them at centers for independent work. You might also send them home for families to work on together with their children. You'll find that these activity sheets are not only fun, but also:

- invite children to respond personally to the book, drawing from their own tastes and experiences
- help children recognize text patterns by repeating those in the book
- allow children to express themselves through drawing as well as writing, catering to different skill levels
- build in scaffolding by providing the spelling of needed words
- help assess comprehension by demonstrating children's understanding of the book's concepts
- and more!

Animal Shape Templates

On pages 40–48, you'll find shape templates of many animals featured in *Guided Science Readers*. Just photocopy, and they're ready to go! Here are just a few ideas for using the templates:

- Stationery – Children can write a letter to their favorite animal!
- Shape books – Children can write facts they learned or their own version of a reader.
- Word walls – Add interest to science vocabulary walls!
- Games – Use them for file-folder and matching games.
- Sorting – Sort the animals by classification.
- And much more!

Guided Science Readers Teaching Guide 7

Tips for Using *Guided Science Readers*

Before Reading

- Introduce the book, giving children a general idea of the topic. Then preview the photographs, inviting children to make predictions about what information they will find, as well as make connections to their own world experiences.
- Encourage children to preview the text as well, and point out a few familiar and unfamiliar words. Discuss strategies they might use to decode unfamiliar words, such as finding beginning and ending sounds, breaking the words into parts, or using the photos as clues.
- Be sure to preview any concepts children may be unfamiliar with before reading the book.

During Reading

- Have children read the book softly to themselves as you circulate, listening in on their reading. While children are reading independently, remember that you are still there to guide them as needed, providing support and scaffolding at appropriate moments.
- If children are having trouble solving a word, guide them to use a helpful strategy. For example, children might look for clues in a photo or use a context clue in a nearby word or phrase. You can provide quiet prompts and encouragement without interrupting the flow of children's reading.
- This is also a good time to assess children's progress, taking note of the skills they use independently and with guidance. Assessment tips and a reproducible rubric are provided on page 10.

After Reading

- First, ask children to respond to the book by telling what they liked most and least about it, and sharing any new things they learned.
- Next, discuss the experience of the reading itself. Encourage children to describe any problems they encountered, then tell how they solved them. You might like to return to those parts of the text that children found challenging, reinforcing word-solving strategies such as using letter-sound spelling relationships.
- This is also a great time for a mini-lesson on word structure. For instance, if a particular book has rhyming words with different spelling patterns (*-eap, -eep*), children can build and sort these words on a magnetic board using magnetic letters.
- You might also do a mini-lesson on fluency by modeling how to use punctuation to guide expression, for instance, by reading a sentence with an exclamation point in a loud, excited tone and having children repeat it after you.
- After your mini-lesson, invite children to reread the book, this time putting their new knowledge to work!

Sample Lesson: *That Bug!* (Level B)

Routine	Example
Introduce the Book	
Display the front cover and talk about it with children.	Read the title aloud and invite children to describe the cover photo.
Preview the book's photos. Stress vocabulary as you point to the corresponding photo.	Discuss each photo. For instance, say: *There is a white butterfly on page 5.* Point to the butterfly and emphasize the word *white*.
Help children tap any prior knowledge they may have on the topic.	Encourage children to share experiences they've had with bugs. Ask: *What bugs have you seen in real life? Where? What did they look like?*
Discuss decoding strategies children can use as they read.	Choose a few words from the book and use them to model how to find beginning and ending sounds, break them into parts, and use photo clues.
Read the Book	
Guide and scaffold children as they read the book.	Have children read quietly to themselves as you listen in.
As necessary, help children use decoding strategies.	Do a think-aloud demonstrating decoding strategies, for instance: *The last word on page 3 starts with* str*. I can say the sound of each letter, and then put them together –* s-t-r *makes* str*. The bee also has stripes on it.* Stripes *starts with* str*. The word must be* stripes!
Check children's comprehension as they read.	Periodically ask questions to monitor children's understanding. For example, you might ask: *Why do you think this book has a grasshopper in it? Does it make sense to you? Why or why not?*
Use the Reproducible	
Photocopy the reproducible that goes with the book and give one to each child.	Read the directions aloud to children. If necessary, model how to complete the activity page by doing one of your own.
Have children complete the activity page independently or with a partner.	Review children's completed activity sheets and discuss their responses. Encourage them to share why they chose that bug, then tell the reasoning behind their descriptive word or phrase.

Assessment

As children use *Guided Science Readers*, there are different reading skills you'll want to keep track of. For example, to track children's decoding skills, take a running record as they read. For each page, record a check mark for every word children read correctly. When children read a word incorrectly, note the correct word as well as its incorrect substitute. When they self-correct, note the strategies they used. Also note any other errors the child makes, such as word omission, insertion, repetition, and so on. It's also important to track comprehension skills. In addition to using the reproducibles, you can also ask children to do an oral retelling of the information they learned from the book.

Of course, one of the best assessment tools a teacher has is his or her own observations. You can take general notes as children read, recording their strengths and challenges, and what strategies may need reinforcement. For more formal assessment, copy the form below and keep one for each child. With these tools, you'll be able to customize your teaching to reach every child—and help all children achieve reading success!

Reading Skills Checklist									
Name									
Date									
Does the child follow the print with his or her eyes (i.e., without using a finger)?									
Does the child recognize most words or use sound-spelling relationships to decode unfamiliar ones?									
Does the child use context clues from surrounding visuals and text to figure out meanings of new words?									
Does the child self-correct by rereading to pronounce difficult words or to improve expression?									
Does the child use appropriate inflections when encountering question marks and interpret other punctuation correctly?									

GRAPHIC ORGANIZER

Name _____

T-Chart

GRAPHIC ORGANIZER

Idea Web

Name _____

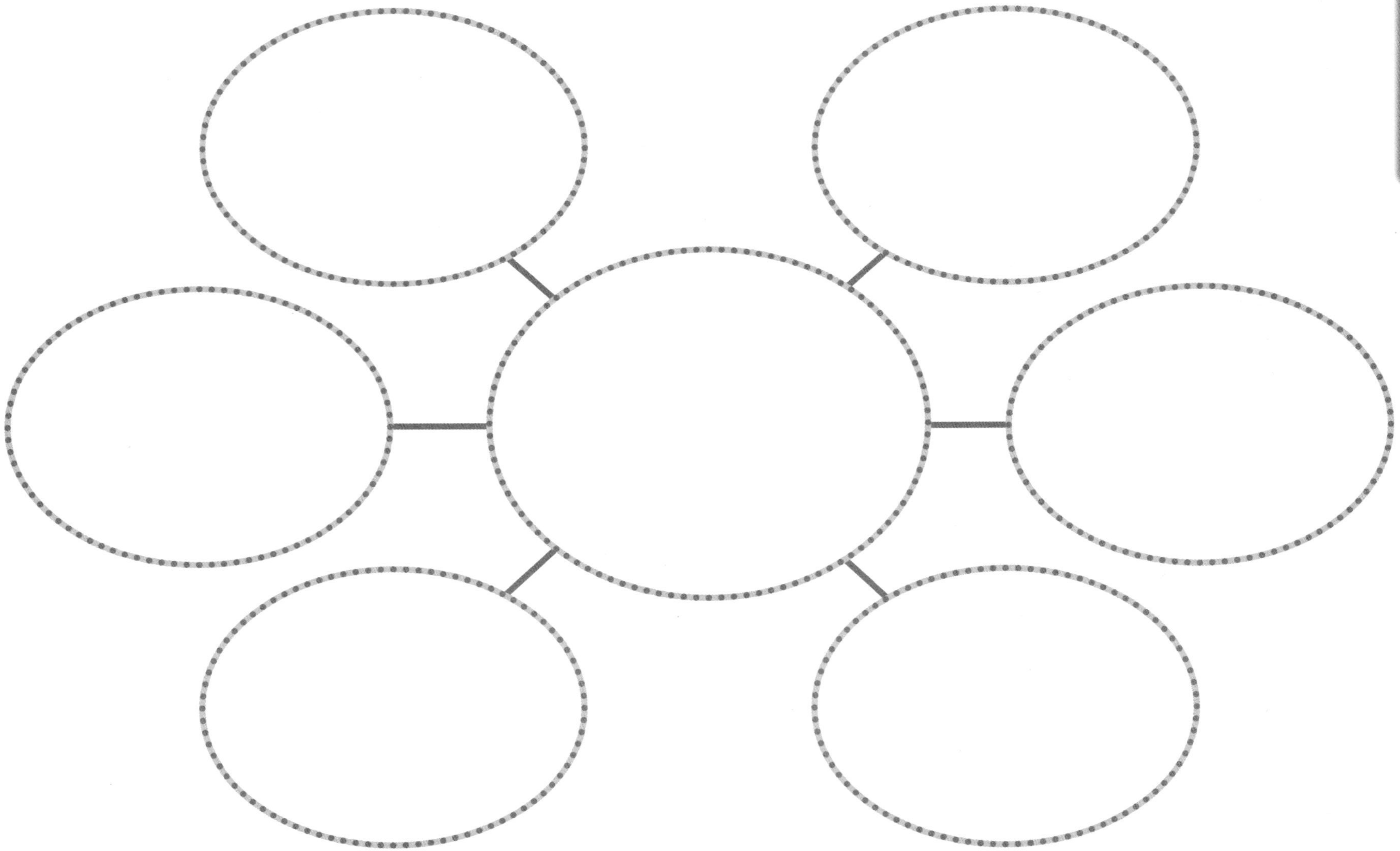

GRAPHIC ORGANIZER

Venn Diagram

Both

Name _____

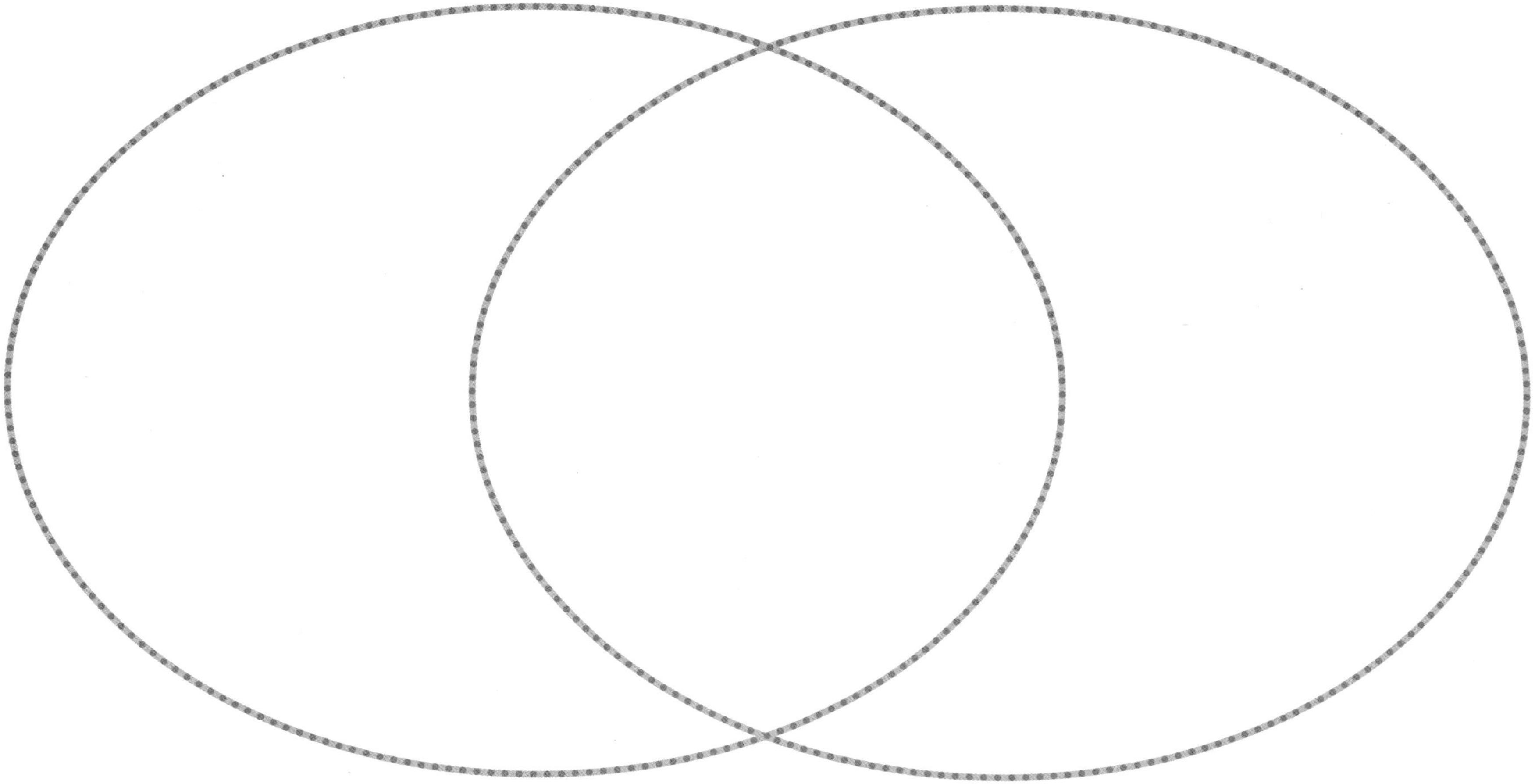

GRAPHIC ORGANIZER

Name _____

Main Idea and Details

Main Idea:

Detail:

Detail:

Detail:

GRAPHIC ORGANIZER

Name _____

KWL Chart

What I **K**now	What I **W**ant to Learn	What I **L**earned

Name _____

Bat Facts

Draw a bat doing something from the book. Then finish the sentence below.

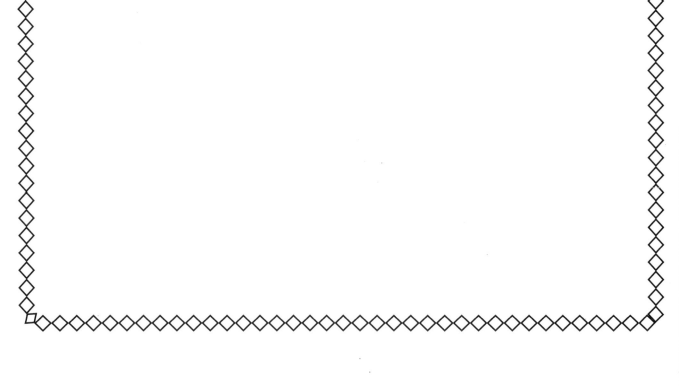

Bats _____.

Name _____

Beautiful Butterflies

Draw a picture of the color butterfly you would like to be. Then finish the sentence below.

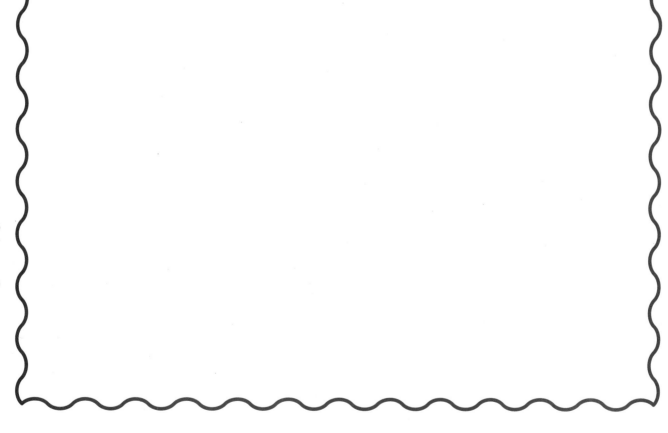

I am _____.

Name _____

Hello, Whale!

Draw a tail and fins on the whale.
Then fill in the letters below.

_____ _____ _____ _____ , whale!

Name _____

A Frog Grows Up

Draw a step from the book about how a frog grows up. Then write a sentence about your picture on the lines below.

Name _____

Penguins Can Go!

Draw something a penguin can do. Then finish the sentence below.

Penguins can _____!

Name _____

Wolf Countdown

Draw a scene from the book. Then write a sentence about your picture on the lines below.

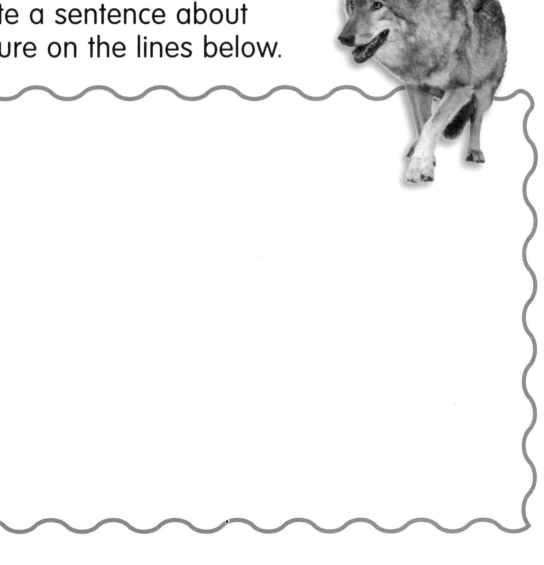

_____

_____

Name _____

Fish Live There!

Draw your favorite fish from the book.

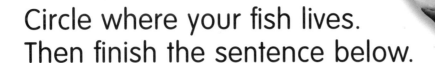

Circle where your fish lives.
Then finish the sentence below.

| river | lake | ocean | fish tank |

My fish lives _____.

Name _____

Meet Some Mammals

Draw two mammals.
Then finish the sentences below.

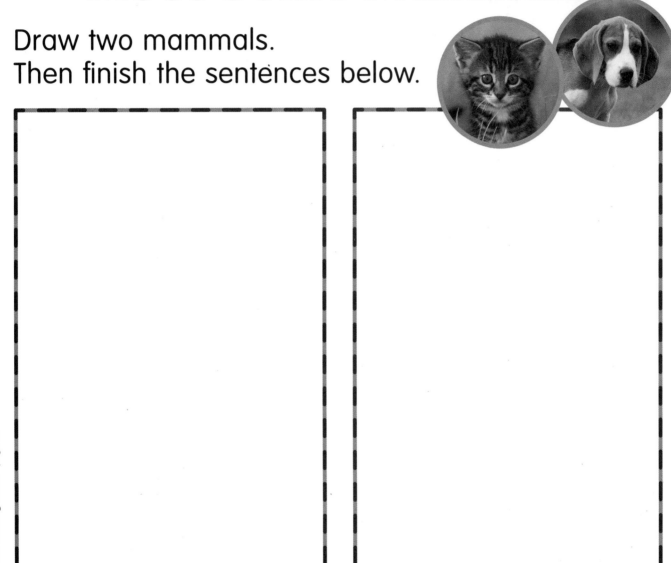

A _____ is a mammal.

A _____ is a mammal, too.

Name _____

Swim, Hop, Crawl

Draw an animal from the book.

Circle what the animal does. Then complete the sentence below. Write what your animal does on all three lines at the bottom.

| swim | hop | crawl |

This is a _____.

_____, _____, _____!

Name _____

See the Reptiles

Draw a reptile. Draw an arrow pointing to a special body part. Then finish the sentence below.

A _____ has _____.

Name _____

That Bug!

Draw your favorite kind of bug. Then finish the sentence below.

My bug is _____.

Name _____

There Is a Bird

Draw a picture of a bird in the nest.
Then finish the sentence below.

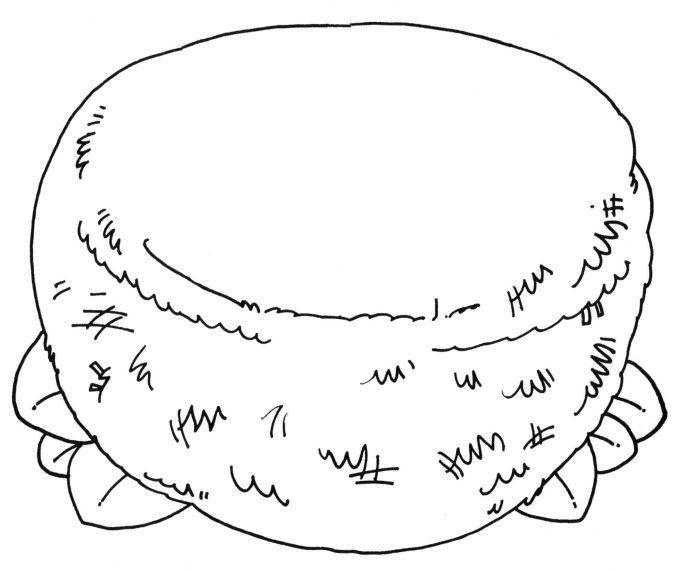

There is a bird in the _____.

Name _____

Desert Animals

Draw a desert animal from the book. Then finish the sentences below.

Let's meet a _____.

It can _____.

Name _____

Farm Friends

Draw a farm animal in the barn.
Then write the sound it makes in the bubble.

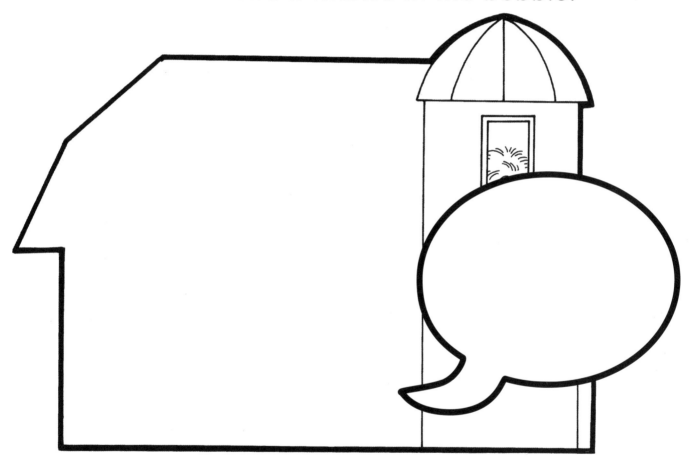

Now finish the sentences below.

A _____ is a farm friend.

It says, "_____!"

Name _____

Forest Animals

Draw a forest animal from the book. Then write a sentence about your picture on the lines below.

Name _____

The Icy, Cold Arctic

Draw an animal that lives in the icy, cold arctic. Then write a sentence about your picture below.

_____

_____

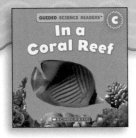

Name _____

In a Coral Reef

Draw an animal from the book. Then finish the sentence below.

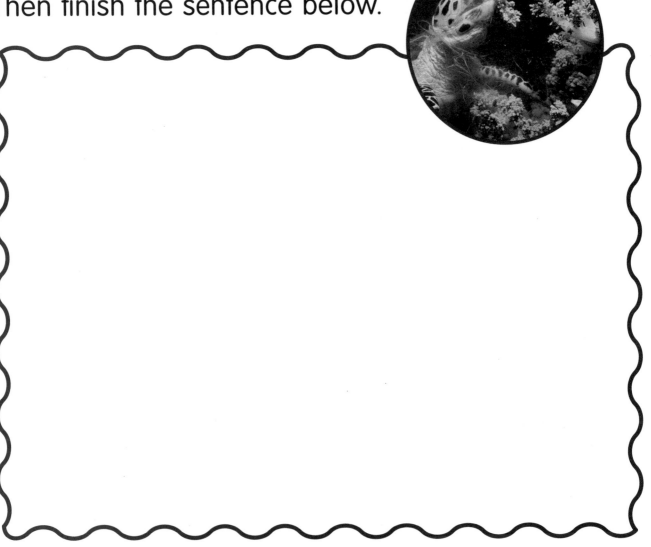

A _____ _____ s

in the busy city.

Name _____

I Spy a Rain Forest

Draw something you might see in a rain forest. Then finish the sentence below.

I spy a _____ in the rain forest.

Name _____

Animal Stars

Finish the picture of the turtle.
Then fill in the letters in the sentences below.

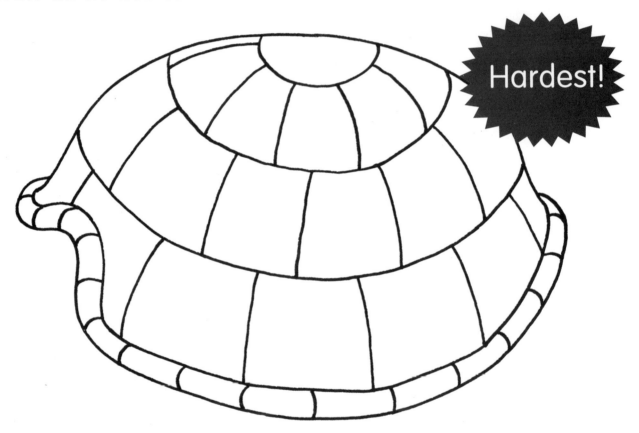

Hardest!

A ____ ____ ____ ____ ____ ____

is an animal star.

It is very ____ ____ ____ ____ ____ !

Name _____

Chicken Life Cycle

Draw a step in the chicken life cycle.
Then write a sentence about your picture below.

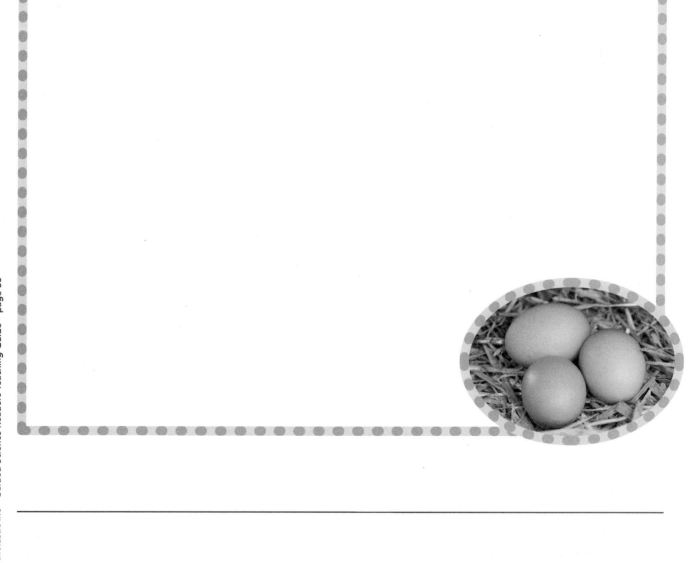

_____

_____

Name _____

Copycat Critters

Draw an animal and its copycat from the book. Then finish the sentence below.

This _____ looks like

a _____.

Hello, copycat!

Name _____

Night Animals

Draw an animal that wakes up at night. Below, write a sentence about your picture.

_____

_____

Name _____

Tails, Tails, Tails!

Draw two animals that have tails.
Then finish the sentence below.

_____ and _____

have tails. Tails, tails, tails!

Name _____

Who Is Hiding?

Draw an animal hiding in the hole.
Then write the animal's name on the sign.

ANIMAL TEMPLATES

Bat, Zebra

ANIMAL TEMPLATES

Frog, Whale

ANIMAL TEMPLATES

Penguin, Wolf

ANIMAL TEMPLATES

Fish, Ladybug

ANIMAL TEMPLATES

Bird, Pig

… ANIMAL TEMPLATES

Rabbit, Polar Bear

ANIMAL TEMPLATES

Octopus, Turtle

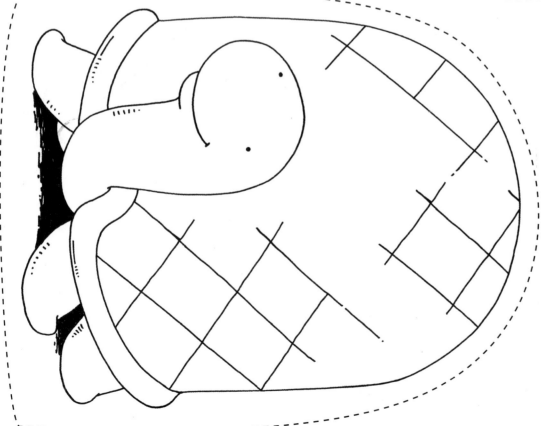

ANIMAL TEMPLATES

Chick, Cow

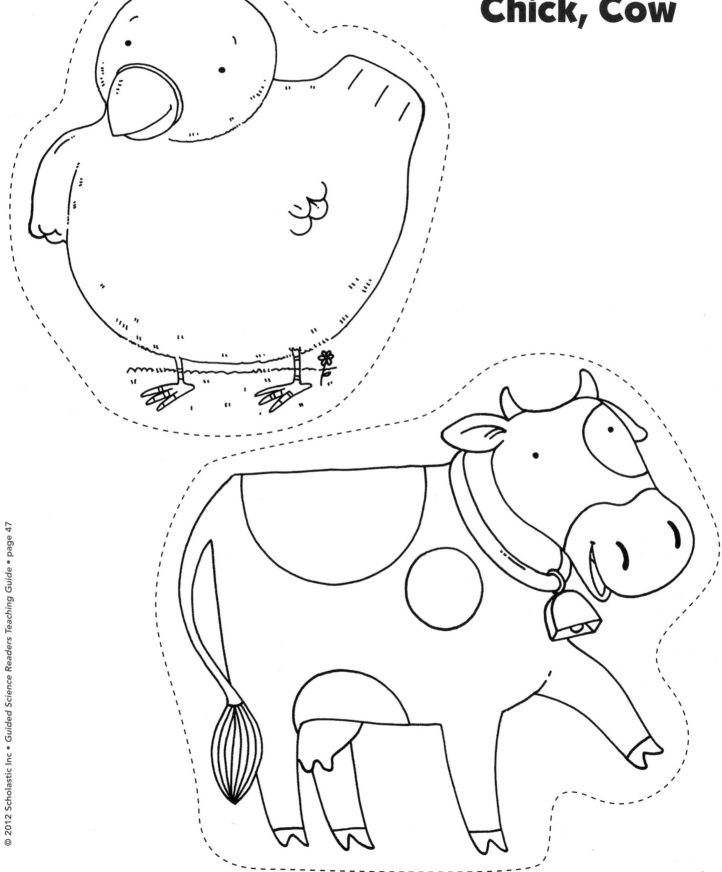

ANIMAL TEMPLATES
Kangaroo, Snake

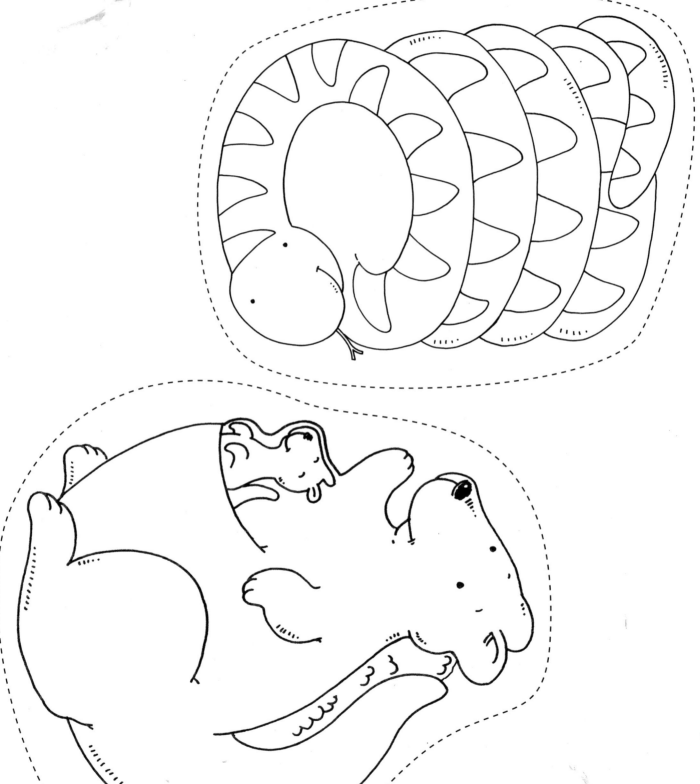